This book belongs to

_____

[NAME]

I will receive the sacrament of reconciliation for the first time on

_____

[DATE]

at

_____

[PARISH]

Your sins are forgiven...

your faith has saved you; go in peace.

LUKE 7:48–50

THIRD PRINTING 2018

TWENTY-THIRD PUBLICATIONS—A Division of Bayard; One Montauk Avenue, Suite 200; New London, CT 06320; (860) 437-3012 or (800) 321-0411; www.twentythirdpublications.com

ISBN: 978-1-62785-008-7

Jesus is always with me

Meet Emily. She is going on a picnic today. Her whole family will be there. A special person named John will be there. John is Emily's cousin. John is a soldier. He has returned home. Everyone wants to welcome John. Everyone is thankful to God that John is home safe.

Someone else will be at the picnic today. Can you guess who it is? Here's a hint: It's someone who loves YOU very much! It's Jesus!

Whenever we gather in love and prayer, Jesus is with us. Jesus is with us when we go to Mass. Jesus loves us so much. He is happy to share everything with us.

SOMETHING TO DO TODAY! Pray for families all over the world.

Draw a picture of your family having a special meal or celebration together. Don't forget to put Jesus in the picture! He is always with you!

Jesus always loves me

❦

Emily is glad John is home safe. Her family prayed for John while he was away. We can't always be with the people we love. But even when they are far away, we don't stop loving them.

It's the same with God. When you were baptized, you became part of God's great big family. No matter where you go or what you do, God always loves you.

Jesus once told a story to show how much he cares for his great big family, even when they are far away.

Jesus said,

"What if you had 100 sheep, but one of them became lost? Wouldn't you leave the 99 in the wilderness and look for the lost one until you found it? And when you found the lost sheep, you would set it on your shoulders with great joy. When you got home, you would call together your friends and neighbors and say, 'Rejoice with me because I have found my lost sheep.'" (Luke 15:4–7)

Jesus is like a loving shepherd who takes good care of his flock. He knows and loves each one of us. He always takes care of us.

How well do you know your sheep?

All the sheep in this family look alike. Some of them are twins! Draw lines to match each sheep with his or her twin brother or sister. Watch out! Some sheep might look alike, but they're not exactly the same!

I thank Jesus for my baptism

Emily is having a lot of fun at the picnic. "This is a perfect day," she says.

Do you remember the story of Adam and Eve? God had created a perfect world for them. But they chose to turn away from God's love. They chose to sin. They were a little like the sheep who wandered away in Jesus' story.

When Adam and Even chose to say "no" to God, things changed. Sadness, suffering, and death came into the good world God had created. We call this "original sin."

SOMETHING TO DO TODAY!

Look at a crucifix or picture of Jesus and say, "Thank you, Jesus, for saving me!"

But remember, God always loves us, no matter what. God never gave up on his people. God sent Jesus to save us from sin.

Through our baptism, we are washed clean of original sin. We can thank Jesus for that! Because of Jesus, we can live in God's goodness and love forever.

6

Does this sound familiar?

Save us, Savior of the world, for by your Cross and Resurrection you have set us free.

We say these words at Mass to show our belief in Jesus' saving power. They are the mystery of our faith.

Here's another way we say this mystery:

*"When we eat this Bread and drink this Cup,
we proclaim your Death, O Lord, until you come again."*

**In the space below, write your own mystery of faith.
It can be as simple as "Jesus, you died for me. I love you."**

_____

_____

_____

_____

God gives us grace

A few days before the picnic, Emily had an idea. "Let's make a sign to welcome John home," she said. Her mom thought that was a great idea. "You decide what the sign will say," Mom said. "Then we'll all paint it together on Saturday."

When Jesus died on the cross, he gave up his life for us. When he rose from the tomb on Easter Sunday, he brought us into new life with God.

When you were baptized, you received a special sign of God's love. It was like a "WELCOME HOME" sign. Baptism marks you forever as God's own child. Baptism wipes away original sin. That means you have a new life with God.

We call this new life grace. Grace is very good because it is God's life and love alive in you.

"BY GRACE you have been saved."

EPHESIANS 2:5

Here's one way to understand grace

Think of something you'd like to draw. Maybe it's something in the room you're in. Maybe it's your best friend. Ready? Okay, now close your eyes and draw the picture in the box below. Keep your eyes closed until you're finished. No peeking!

Once you've opened your eyes, look at your picture.
Now draw the same picture below,
but this time with your eyes open.

Big difference, huh?

Grace is a gift from God that helps us see the way to live in faith, hope, and love. Grace gives us strength to be signs of Jesus' love for the whole world.

God lets me choose

⟨⟩

"I know Mom said to wait until Saturday," Emily thought. "But I really want to make John's sign today." She found a roll of paper and some paint. Emily painted some letters, but the sign didn't look right. Emily reached for more paint. Oops. Emily spilled paint on the rug. She knew her mom would be unhappy. So Emily did something else. She hid the rug and the sign under her bed.

"Where is my rug?" Emily's mom asked later. Emily said she didn't know. Uh-oh.

God doesn't tell us what to do. God wants us to choose his way of love, but sometimes we don't. Sometimes we turn away from God's love and grace. We choose to sin. When we sin, we hurt our friendship with God and with others. That just doesn't feel good.

SOMETHING TO DO TODAY! Here's a good prayer to learn: *O Lord Jesus Christ, Son of God, have mercy on me, a sinner.*

Below you'll find some qualities
of a loving person. To the right of each word,
you'll see its opposite. In the spaces below,
write down the words that describe you.

Loving   Unloving

kind ·················· selfish

helpful ·················· lazy

fair ·················· playing favorites

trustworthy ·················· lying

friendly ·················· snobbish

respectful ·················· bossy

happy ·················· grumpy

honest ·················· dishonest

thankful ·················· ungrateful

forgiving ·················· holding a grudge

Here are some loving
qualities that describe me:

_____

_____

_____

Here are some unloving
qualities I will work on:

_____

_____

_____

Everybody sins

Emily felt terrible. She could barely eat her dinner. She couldn't sleep. The next morning, Emily talked to her mom. Emily showed her the rug and the sign. Emily said she was very sorry. Emily's mom said she could tell that Emily was truly sorry, and she forgave Emily. She showed Emily how to wash the paint out of the rug.

SOMETHING TO DO TODAY!

Think about a time you chose to turn away from God's goodness and love. Ask for God's forgiveness.

A **mortal sin** is a serious sin that can cut us off from God's love. A **venial sin** is less serious, but it can still weaken our relationship with God.

Remember when we said that Jesus is always with us?
It's true. He's with us when he forgives us in a certain
SACRAMENT. Do you know what it is? To find out, break
the code by writing what the pictures are. Then put the circled
letters together to find out how Jesus is with us.

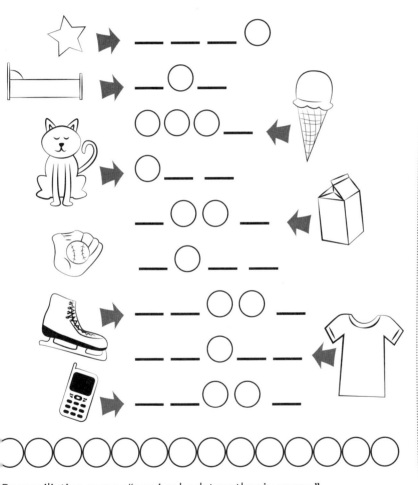

Reconciliation means "coming back together in peace."
When we sin, we turn away from God, but in the sacrament of
reconciliation, God brings us back to him, just like the lost sheep.

Here's a story Jesus told his friends to help them understand how God forgives us, even when we turn away from him.

Once, a young man ran away from home. He lived foolishly and spent all his dad's money. When all the money was gone, he was poor and hungry. So he got a job feeding pigs.

He was so hungry he wished he could eat the food he fed to the pigs! But nobody even gave him that.

Finally he thought, "My father's workers have more food to eat than I do. I am dying of hunger. I will go to my father and say, 'Father, I have sinned against heaven and against you. I am not fit to be called your son; treat me like one of your hired workers.'"

So he got up and returned to his father. While he was still a long way off, his father caught sight of him and was filled with love. He ran to his son, hugged him, and kissed him.

His son said, "Father, I have sinned against heaven and against you; I am not fit to be called your son."

But his father ordered his servants, "Quickly bring the finest robe and put it on him; put a ring on his finger and sandals on his feet. Let's have a big feast, because this son of mine was dead, and has come to life again; he was lost, and has been found." Then the celebration began.

(BASED ON LUKE 15:11-24)

14

Put the pictures from this story in the right order:

I am sorry for my sins

The paint had dried, so Emily had to work hard to clean the rug. She scrubbed and rinsed. Then she scrubbed some more. "I'll never get it all out," Emily moaned.

Emily couldn't clean all the paint out. Some things are just impossible. But for God, nothing is impossible! When we confess our sins in the sacrament of reconciliation, God forgives us. Our sins are wiped away forever. There isn't a speck left!

Contrition means being sorry. We receive God's forgiveness when we are sorry for our sins.

THE WAY TO FORGIVENESS IN THE SACRAMENT OF RECONCILIATION

1 We admit we were wrong.

2 We say we are sorry.

3 We ask God's forgiveness.

4 We promise to do better next time.

5 We make up for our sin as best we can. (In the sacrament of reconciliation, a priest gives us a penance. A penance is something we do or prayers to say that can help make up for what we've done.)

Each of the rocks has one step to forgiveness on it. But, uh-oh, Larry Lamb has mixed up the rocks. Help him put them back in order by writing the right numbers on the rocks.

I celebrate reconciliation with God ∽

On Saturday, Emily's family made a new sign for John. Everyone helped, even Emily's little brother. They brought the sign to the picnic. John loved the sign. "Thanks for making me feel welcome," John said.

Reconciliation is a sign of God's love. It's a celebration too.

When Jesus died on the cross his friends were sad and afraid. But on Easter Sunday, when Jesus rose from the dead, his friends saw him. They were full of joy.

Because so many great things happen in the sacrament of reconciliation, we celebrate it! There are many names for this celebration: We call it Confession because we confess our sins. We call it Reconciliation because we come back to God's love. We call it Penance because we do something to make up for our sins. (For instance, we might say prayers or do acts of kindness.)

SOMETHING TO DO TODAY!

18

You've learned a lot of new words. Here's a crossword to help you remember them.

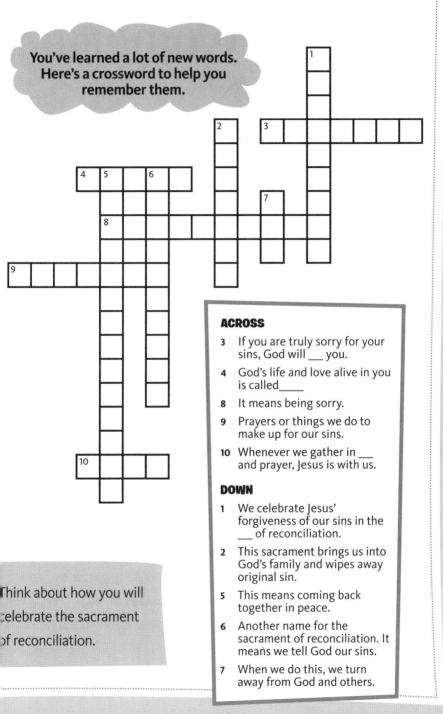

ACROSS

3 If you are truly sorry for your sins, God will ___ you.

4 God's life and love alive in you is called____

8 It means being sorry.

9 Prayers or things we do to make up for our sins.

10 Whenever we gather in ___ and prayer, Jesus is with us.

DOWN

1 We celebrate Jesus' forgiveness of our sins in the ___ of reconciliation.

2 This sacrament brings us into God's family and wipes away original sin.

5 This means coming back together in peace.

6 Another name for the sacrament of reconciliation. It means we tell God our sins.

7 When we do this, we turn away from God and others.

Think about how you will celebrate the sacrament of reconciliation.

I forgive others

At the picnic, Emily's little brother spills pink lemonade on her new sneakers. Emily gets kind of mad. Then Emily remembers how her mom forgave her. Emily forgives her brother right away. She remembers how much she loves her brother. She gives him a big hug. "This is the best day ever," she says.

Once, Saint Peter wanted to know how many times he should forgive someone who had wronged him. He asked Jesus, "Should I forgive my brother as many as seven times?" Jesus answered, "I say to you, not seven times but seventy-seven times." (Matthew 18:21–22)

Jesus said this to show that there's no limit on how many times we forgive others, because there's no limit on how many times God our Father forgives us.

In the Our Father prayer, we say, "Forgive us our trespasses as we forgive those who trespass against us." When we remember that God always forgives our sins, it's a little easier to forgive others.

SOMETHING TO DO TODAY!

Say the Our Father. When you get to the part about "forgive us our trespasses," try saying "forgive me my trespasses as I forgive those who trespass against me."

Larry Lamb's brother Lee broke Larry's favorite toy. Lee is very sorry. What should Larry do? Follow the maze.

I live by good rules

At the picnic, Emily sees her cousins playing a game. They are throwing rings around a stake in the ground. "It's called horseshoes," says her cousin John. "Come on, I'll show you how to play."

What's your favorite game? Imagine trying to play a game like baseball, or tag, or Simon Says—without any rules. How would you know who was "it"? How would you know where to throw the ball? Rules help everyone know how to play so we can all have fun.

Long ago, God gave us the Ten Commandments. These are rules that help us live our lives.

1 I, the Lord, am your God; You shall not have other gods besides me
2 You shall not take the name of the Lord God in vain
3 Remember to keep holy the Lord's Day
4 Honor your father and your mother
5 You shall not kill
6 You shall not commit adultery
7 You shall not steal
8 You shall not bear false witness
9 You shall not covet your neighbor's wife
10 You shall not covet your neighbor's goods

Here's an easy game with a few simple rules. All you need is a penny to play. Toss the penny to see how far you can move. Heads moves you forward one square. Tails moves you forward two squares. You can play this game alone or with a friend. The first one to the finish line wins.

Your best friend is sick. You brought him his homework. **MOVE AHEAD 2 SPACES.**			You kept a book from your class library instead of returning it. **MOVE BACK 2 SPACES.**	**finish!**
				You fed the dog without being asked. **MOVE AHEAD 3 SPACES.**
You took extra cookies from the kitchen and blamed your brother. **GO BACK TO START.**			You told your mom you brushed your teeth, but you didn't. **MOVE BACK 2 SPACES.**	
		Some kids at school used bad words, but you chose not to. **MOVE AHEAD 1 SPACE.**		
start	You went to church on Sunday. **MOVE AHEAD 1 SPACE.**		You didn't pay attention during Father's homily. **MOVE BACK 1 SPACE.**	

❧ Sometimes I need help making choices

Emily has made some choices. Some were good. Some weren't so good.

Here's a story about a choice Saint Peter made. On the night before Jesus died, he told Peter something. Jesus said that before the rooster crowed in the morning, Peter would pretend three times that he didn't know Jesus. Peter was shocked. "Lord, I am prepared to go to prison and to die with you," he said. But when the soldiers came and took Jesus away, Peter kept far behind. When Peter got to the place where Jesus was being held, he stayed outside, warming his hands by the fire.

A servant stared at Peter. "This man was with Jesus," she said. But Peter said, "I don't know him." Someone else saw Peter and said, "You too are one of them."
But Peter said, "I am not."
An hour later, someone else said, "Yes, this man was with Jesus. He is from the same town." But Peter said, "I do not know what you are talking about." Just as he spoke, the rooster crowed. Jesus turned and looked at Peter.
Peter remembered what Jesus had said. Peter felt so awful about what he'd done that he went out and cried.
(BASED ON LUKE 22:33–34, 54–62)

Peter made some good choices in his life, but this was NOT one of them. How do we know how to make good choices? It's not always easy. Of course, we have the Ten Commandments. And God's grace. But sometimes, making good choices isn't easy.

When you have a tough choice to make, just remember to **STOP**.

S Stop for a moment and think about your choice. Does it show love for God and others?

T Think about what will happen if you make your choice. Could it hurt you or someone else?

O Okay? Is your choice okay with God's laws?

P Pray to the Holy Spirit for help.

Try using **STOP** to decide what to do here. Write your choice on the lines below.

You're at a friend's house. Your friend wants to watch a TV show you're not allowed to watch. What do you do?

_____

_____

_____

_____

_____

_____

_____

SOMETHING TO DO TODAY!

Think about some choices you've made this week. Did you make good or bad choices? How did you feel after any bad choices you made? How about the good ones?

I look at my own life

Emily is receiving the sacrament of reconciliation in a few weeks. She is learning how to go confession, just like you are.

Emily is learning about conscience. Our conscience (CON-shenz) is a gift from God that helps us tell right from wrong. To get ready for confession, we think about things we have done wrong. This is called an examination of conscience.

One way of doing this is to think about the Ten Commandments. We look at them and see how we measure up.

Jesus also gave us the Beatitudes (bee-AT-it-toods) to teach us how to love God and others. We can also use the Beatitudes to help us get ready for confession. For instance:

Jesus says, "Blessed are the poor in spirit. The kingdom of heaven is theirs." We are poor in spirit when we remember how much we need God. Ask yourself: Do I turn to God when I need help? Do I follow his laws? Jesus also says, "Blessed are the sorrowful. They will be comforted." Ask yourself: Do I help those who are sad? Do I cause anyone to be hurt by my actions?

Think of a time you didn't follow Jesus' way of loving and living. Write a prayer to ask his forgiveness.

Dear Jesus,

_____

_____

_____

_____

_____

_____

_____

_____

_____

I go to confession

When Emily makes her first confession in a few weeks, she will go to church with her family. She will talk to Father Dave. But really, she will be talking to Jesus, because Jesus is present in this sacrament. It is Jesus who forgives our sins, through the priest.

When we receive the sacrament of reconciliation, we say certain things in a certain order. That's called a rite. The rite of reconciliation isn't too hard. Still, sometimes we forget what to say! But we don't have to worry because the priest always helps us.

SOMETHING TO DO TODAY!
Practice going to confession. Think about what you will say and do.

Here's how we go to confession. As you color each picture, think about the words and how you will say them when you go to confession.

I celebrate God's forgiveness ∽ and love ∾

Emily's dad says that after Emily receives the sacrament of reconciliation, they will do something fun to celebrate God's love and forgiveness. Can you guess how Emily wants to celebrate? Hint: There will be cake and lots of games!

We celebrate Jesus' forgiveness and love every time we go to Mass. We do this in our prayers when we say, "Lord, have mercy." We do this when we receive Jesus in Holy Communion.

When you receive the sacrament of reconciliation, you will be one step closer to receiving Jesus in Holy Communion. Now that's something to celebrate!

Jesus says, "I am the living bread that came down from heaven; whoever eats this bread will live forever; and the bread that I will give is my flesh for the life of the world." (John 6:51)

Amen!

Make a list of things you are thankful for. Don't forget Jesus' forgiveness and love!

SOMETHING TO DO TODAY!

Celebrate God's love for you by saying a prayer of praise, such as, "Thank you, Lord, for reconciliation!"

_____

_____

_____

_____

_____

_____

_____

_____

_____

_____

_____

_____

_____

Prayers I Know

Sign of the Cross
In the name of the Father and of the
Son and of the Holy Spirit. Amen.

Act of Contrition
My God, I am sorry for my sins with all my heart.
In choosing to do wrong and failing to do good, I
have sinned against you whom I should love above
all things. I firmly intend, with your help, to do
penance, to sin no more, and to avoid whatever
leads me to sin. Our Savior Jesus Christ suffered
and died for us. In his name, my God, have mercy.

The Lord's Prayer
Our Father, who art in heaven, hallowed
    be thy name; thy kingdom come;
thy will be done on earth as it is in heaven.
    Give us this day our daily bread;
and forgive us our trespasses as we forgive
    those who trespass against us;
and lead us not into temptation,
    but deliver us from evil. Amen.

Glory Be to the Father
Glory be to the Father, and to the Son, and to the
    Holy Spirit; as it was in the beginning, is now,
    and ever shall be, world without end. Amen.